Words I Use When I Write

by

Alana Trisler
Patrice Howe Cardiel

ISBN 0-935493-33-6
Words I Use When I Write.

Item No.466

To Beth —
our friend and mentor

A.T.
P.H.C.

A a

a
about
after
again
airplane
all
along
also
always
am
an
and

animal
another
any
apple
are
around
as
ask
at
ate
away

Aa

B b

baby	big
back	black
ball	blue
bat	book
be	both
beautiful	boy
because	box
bed	bring
been	brother
before	brown
best	but
better	buy

Bb

by

C c

call
came
can
car
carry
cat
chair
children

Christmas
city
clean
coat
cold
come
coming
could
country
cow
cut

C c

Cc

C c

D d

daddy   down

day   draw

dear   dress

did   drink

didn't

dinosaur

do

does

dog

done

don't

door

D d

Ee

each _____

ear _____

eat _____

egg

eight

elephant

end

enough

ever _____

every _____

eye _____

E e

Ff

fall

far

fast

father

favorite

few

find

fine

fire

first

five

fly

for

found

four

friend

from

full

fun

funny

4

F f

Gg

game   goes
gave   going
get   good
girl   got
give   grade
glad   green
go   grow

Gg

Hh

had

hair

hand

happy her

hard   here

has   him

hat   his

have   hold

he   holiday

head   home

heard hope

help   horse

Hh

hot

house

how

hug

hurt

I i

I
ice cream
if
in
into
is
it
its

I i

J j

jump
jumprope
just

K k

kangaroo   know
keep
kind
king
kite

J j

K k

Ll

large	look
last	
laugh	
leaf	
left	
let	
letter	
light	
like	
little	
live	
long	

M m

made

make

man

many

may

me

men

milk

money

moon

more

morning

most

mother

mouth

much

must

my

myself

_____

_____

M m

N n

name

needle

never

new

next

nice

night

no

nobody

nose

not

now

number

Nn

O o

of

off

often

old

on

once

one

only

open

or

orange

other

our

out

outside

over

own

_____

_____

_____

Oo

P p

paper
party
pass
past
pay
pencil
people
pet
pick
pig
place
play

please
pretty
pull
put

_____

_____

_____

Pp

Q q

quick

quiet

queen

question

Qq

Rr

rabbit	ride
race	right
rain	rocket
ran	room
read	round
ready	run
red	

_____

_____

_____

_____

_____

Rr

S s

said	sing
saw	sister
say	sit
school	six
scissors	sleep
see	small
seven	so
shall	some
she	something
should	soon
show	spelling
side	spring

S s

start
stay
stop
story
street
summer
sun
sure

S s

S s

Tt

take	them
talk	then
teacher	there
telephone	these
television	they
tell	thing
ten	think
than	this
thank	those
that	thought
the	three
their	through

T t

time _____

to _____

today _____

together _____

told _____

too _____

took _____

town _____

try _____

two _____

_____ _____

_____ _____

T+

U u

umbrella	us
under	use
until	used
up	
upon	

V v

valentine

vase

very

volcano

I love you!

U u

V v

W w

walk	were
want	what
warm	when
was	where
wash	which
watch	while
water	white
way	who
we	why
week	will
well	winter
went	wish

W w

with
work
would
write

X x

x-ray

_____

_____

Y y

yard   you
yarn   your
year
yellow
yes

X x

Y y

Z z

zero   zipper

zig-zag   zoo

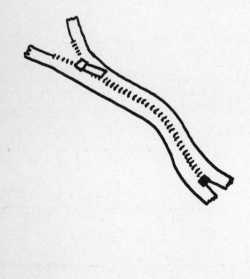

Color Words

black _____

blue _____

brown _____

green _____

orange _____

purple _____

red _____

white _____

yellow _____

_____ _____

_____ _____

Contractions

aren't	are not
can't	cannot
didn't	did not
doesn't	does not
don't	do not
I'll	I will
I'm	I am
isn't	is not
it's	it is
I've	I have
let's	let us
wasn't	was not

Contractions

we're	we are
won't	will not
you're	you are

_____   _____

_____   _____

_____   _____

_____   _____

_____   _____

_____   _____

_____   _____

Days of the Week

Sunday	Sun.
Monday	Mon.
Tuesday	Tues.
Wednesday	Wed.
Thursday	Thurs.
Friday	Fri.
Saturday	Sat.

Months of the Year

January	Jan.
February	Feb.
March	Mar.
April	Apr.
May	
June	
July	
August	Aug.
September	Sept.
October	Oct.
November	Nov.
December	Dec.

Number Words

one	eleven
two	twelve
three	thirteen
four	fourteen
five	fifteen
six	sixteen
seven	seventeen
eight	eighteen
nine	nineteen
ten	twenty

Ordinal Numbers

first	eleventh
second	twelfth
third	thirteenth
fourth	fourteenth
fifth	fifteenth
sixth	sixteenth
seventh	seventeenth
eighth	eighteenth
ninth	nineteenth
tenth	twentieth

Classmates...
and Friends

_____   _____

_____   _____

_____   _____

_____   _____

_____   _____

_____   _____

_____   _____

_____   _____

_____   _____

Family

Pets